The children were in the sea.

1

They played in the waves.

Dad made them laugh.

Everyone was cold.

Kipper was very cold.

Everyone wanted to jog.

6

Kipper sat on the rug.

'Come on, Kipper,' said Mum.

8

'I'm too cold,' said Kipper.

'Come on, Kipper,' said Dad.

'I'm too cold,' said Kipper.

'Come and help,' said everyone.

'I'm too cold,' said Kipper.

'Ice cream!' said Kipper.

14

He ran to the van.

Everyone looked at Kipper.
'I'm not that cold,' he said.